I0484102

# ZAP YOUR PROCRASTINATION

## HOW TO STOP BEING LAZY AND GET RESULTS IN YOUR LIFE

# Contents

# WILL THIS BOOK HELP ME?

If you have a to-do list as long as your arm and you are struggling with the workload, this book will help.

If you geek out on productivity techniques (like me :)), this book will give you a simple system to tie it all together.

Do you feel like you are stuck in a rut? This book will help you make simple changes to your life to help you get unstuck.

If you need a beginner's guide to productivity, this book will help you jump-start your productivity.

You are probably reading this book because:

- You are finding it difficult to get motivated and

stay motivated.

- You want more; you don't want a mediocre life with mediocre results!

- You want to make lasting changes in your life.

- You would like to get rid of your self-sabotaging ways once and for all.

When I began to write this book, I simply wrote out the fifteener method with a few examples and thought I was done. However, after reading the draft a few times, I realized that I had made some critical assumptions about you. The reason these assumptions are critical is because if they happen to be wrong, then this whole book would be rendered useless. I have listed out my assumptions below to ensure that we are on the same page.

(1) I assume you are reading this book because you have a goal in mind, something that defines your life. Something that not only challenges you, but also excites you.

(2) I also assume that you realize the importance of creating habits — specifically, habits that take you towards this goal.

(3) I assume that you can take the framework suggested and run with it; that is, you would be able to customize the framework to fit your life.

(4) While outlining the fifteener system, I will also

assume that you are attempting to push the limits of your core skills and not trying to do things that are not part of your core or beyond your current skills.

I would like to believe that I can help you achieve this goal, but I struggle with the fact that I don't know your goals, and I also don't know if my method will fit your life. But, you can rest assured for two reasons:

**1. You won't have to start this journey alone**. I have created a website, www.7bigrocks.com, where you will have access to additional information, templates, and free downloads to help take this forward.

**2. You can always reach out to me by sending me an email.** My email address is 7bigrocks@gmail.com.

# INTRODUCTION

"Procrastination is the thief of time."
— Edward Young

I cannot claim to be an expert on productivity, but I can definitely claim to be an expert on procrastination, since I have done so much of it :).

In my previous book, *CrazyBusy*, I outlined a weekly review system (The 7 Big Rocks Weekly Review System) that helped me get out of the rut I was in. It helped me to review the week gone by as well as plan for the coming week so that I could have a better handle on things. Over time, this system became the reason for my own personal growth.

But I wish I could claim it was a "perfect system." In reality, there were parts of the system that I have had to refine over many years. Other parts simply did not work and I had to get rid of them.

In order to understand this further, I would have to take you back to the time when I first started implementing the 7 Big Rocks Weekly Review System.

The first four weeks of the weekly review were flawless. I had so many things that needed to be done each and every week that I found myself looking forward to my weekly review, and I laid out a perfect plan week after week. My productivity level was high.

It was the fifth week that surprised me. I'd finished my review on a Sunday. I had planned out a very deliberate, well-focused, profitable, and meaningful week. I was a bit smug in my attitude, knowing I'd found a system that actually worked. I patted myself on the back for identifying one more set of victories for the week ahead and was already looking forward to repeating my success in the coming week.

Then came Monday morning.

It began with just a few sniffles, then escalated to a fever, and then ended up with me spending two days in bed. Finally, by Thursday, I got back into action. I thought, "No problem," as I looked over all the things that I missed getting done over that three-day period. After all, there were still four more days left in this week!

The following Sunday, as I was doing my weekly review, it hit me. My productivity was at an all-time low. I had accomplished little this entire week, and nothing that mattered or was specifically worth mentioning. I was, to say the least, disappointed. My "perfect" system had not worked. I was down on myself for how smug I'd been. I tried to console myself by reminding myself that I had been sick, but I vowed to make up for it in the following week.

To my great surprise, the following week was just as empty and disappointing. This time, I had no excuse, because my health had been perfectly fine for the entire seven-day week. Now I was in agony, wondering what I was doing wrong. As I mulled it over, I finally realized that the past two weeks were slightly different from the first four weeks. Here are those differences:

(1) I had been low on energy.
(2) I'd lost momentum.
(3) My attention span was reduced.
(4) My decision-making was ineffective because there were too many decisions to make.
(5) I had lost my motivation in the sixth week and I started procrastinating.

I decided to take some time off and give this some careful study. I spent most of that time writing. While poring over my notes, a few things jumped out at me. I realized that what I really needed was:

(a) Both a short-term and a long-term system
(b) To try to mix it up a little
(c) To be prepared to face unexpected obstacles

The real key to this revelation was realizing that I needed more than just ONE system. I needed several systems all working together simultaneously, like one giant ecosystem to ensure my outcomes would be predictable every week. So I came up with quite a few different little mini-systems. Some of these mini-systems worked, and some did not, but my productivity increased by leaps and bounds.

One of these mini-systems happened to be the 7 Big Rocks Fifteener System, which I am outlining in this book. I came up with this system specifically to beat procrastination and to eliminate time-consuming decisions wherever possible.

It all started when I realized that it was not just the outcome, the end result that I wanted to achieve, that was important, but also the process of how I achieved it. The way I achieved it was by maintaining a new, more solid system of checklists to help me eliminate all the decision-making when it was time to execute my plan.

### Not another Checklist book!

The whole purpose of writing this book is definitely not to convince you to write more checklists. I believe you already know that checklists are a vital part of being productive. It is my goal to help you create a fall-back system that you can implement easily when you're feeling a little overwhelmed with all the decision-making. You should focus only on the execution of your plan. Using this strategy, you never have to worry about deciding what you'll do next, because all you need to do is refer to your checklist and follow that plan.

The 7 Big Rocks Fifteener System shows you how to master your focus by making a simple commitment of 15 minutes a day. Fifteen-minute routines are what this book is all about. Also, the system is scalable, so if you want to do two fifteen-minute routines for a total of 30 minutes a day, that is fine, too.

Productivity depends on executing important tasks in line with your goals. However, no matter how positive the transformation, you will inevitably encounter some form of resistance. There is an inner saboteur inside each of us, whom I refer to as the "Procrastination Devil." It is important to understand that everyone procrastinates, and identifying the reasons for that is the key to overcoming it.

Procrastination doesn't need to rule your life. Much like any good military commander seeks to understand his opponent as best as possible in order to gain victory, you should attempt to have as much knowledge as possible about what is causing you to procrastinate.

# TYPES OF PROCRASTINATION

I have tried to list the top reasons why people procrastinate. I get the fact that this is not a comprehensive list; however, understanding these reasons has given me a new perspective on how to put an end to my own procrastination.

As per Wikipedia, "Procrastination is the practice of carrying out less urgent tasks in preference to more urgent ones, or doing more pleasurable things in place of less pleasurable ones, and thus putting off impending tasks to a later time, sometimes to the 'last minute' before the deadline."

I would like to help you, the reader, identify the red flags for each type of procrastination and hopefully, with the right knowledge, you will be able to train yourself to beat procrastination and find your inner focus and motivation. The more you know about why you procrastinate, the easier it becomes to zap the Procrastination Devil.

Without further ado, let's dive into the list and try to understand what is causing you to procrastinate.

### Reason 1: Lack of motivation or lack of interest

No one I know feels motivated and energized by the prospect of mowing the lawn, raking leaves, or doing taxes! Tasks that are viewed as being unpleasant are often the victim of procrastination. While many people will tackle a task that they enjoy with relish, they may consistently delay working on tasks they view as less appealing.

Lack of interest also seems to play a role in procrastination. All students from time to time lack interest in a course, but not all of these students delay studying or completing assignments.

I myself procrastinate doing my tax returns. If you know a job has to be done, but it's not emotionally important to you, find a way to make it important. In my case, the prospect of a tax refund has me sitting down with my calculator pretty quick.

Another strategy involves taking an attitude check. Some people only do things they like doing and procrastinate on things they don't like. Ask yourself: "Does my attitude prevent me from being motivated?" If your answer is "yes," then it is time to figure a way to make an attitude adjustment. This may mean finding someone else to do part of the unpleasant task (if it does not cost too much) or it may mean simply changing your attitude. It may also mean re-evaluating your goals and determining which "steps" do or do not fit into the larger picture. If succeeding in the boring finance class seems to be a necessary step toward achieving your larger goals, that fact alone may motivate you.

Yet another strategy is the prospect of a reward. Sometimes it helps to promise yourself a reward for doing your taxes. As an example, I promised myself a reward: Out of the tax refund, I would buy myself a bicycle, something I'd been thinking about for a while to help me get back in shape.

Identify the reason for the procrastination. Confront your attitudes and fears. Weigh the consequences. Re-frame your mindset.

Then deal with it!

## Reason 2: You haven't really committed to doing the task

Sometimes we do things because someone else wants us to do them, and other times we delay things because someone else wants us to do them.

*"I" have not personally committed to doing this task, therefore I tend to procrastinate.*

Do you know anybody who got into the family bakery business, or became a lawyer, or joined the Marines because someone else expected or demanded it? If so, you probably know an unhappy baker or lawyer or Marine.

We need to differentiate between commitment and involvement. While they seem to be similar concepts, in reality, they are poles apart.

You may chronically put off an activity because you aren't really committed to it at all. If you can figure out your own reasons for doing the job, that would make it easier for you to commit to the task fully and therefore it would be easier to execute.

However, if you can find no internal motivation, no benefit for doing the job, and no penalty for not doing it, you may well decide not to do it at all. In that case, do what you have to do to get out of the task. That's not the same thing as simply putting it off. This is a definitive decision not to do the task and to accept the consequences, if any. In the long run, that sort of decision costs less in terms of time and stress than does the passive resistance of procrastination.

### Rebellion and laziness

Another common cause of procrastination is what Seth Godin refers to as the "lizard brain." What he is referring to is our irrational, internal resistance when we say we want one thing and then go and do something else. It is the tendency to do something completely different even though we know what we ought to be doing.

Delaying tactics can be a form of rebellion against imposed schedules, standards, and expectations. The expectations are often those of a power struggle, but at a subconscious level. This is closely related to a lack of commitment.

Rebellion and resistance are reactions, not actions; thus, the control of your behavior rests with whatever or whomever you are rebelling or resisting against. If you are rebelling against your parents or some other authority figure, then they have a great deal of power in your life — probably more than you are willing to admit.

## Reason 3: Complexity and lack of knowledge

You look at a task at hand and feel helpless. It may actually be a daunting task at your current skill level. You then try to avoid the task because it seems too complex.

The fact is that you may simply not know enough to do the job right. You haven't consciously recognized or admitted this to yourself, but you know it deep down, and your mind starts playing tricks on you.

The inability to make decisions also contributes to procrastination. Many people simply spend too much time trying to make decisions about their projects. While it is important to weigh your options carefully and make informed decisions, too much time spent wastefully trying to make a decision can cause a significant delay for a project.

Sometimes, it is helpful to recall one of your previous successes with conquering a complex task, just to get yourself in a positive mindset. Think of a time you were really on top of things, achieving great results — when you were "in the zone" — and say to yourself, "If I could do it then, I can definitely do it now."

You might need to set aside some time each day specifically for the purpose of making decisions and set a timeline for yourself to complete the decision-making process. This will encourage you to use your time wisely and reach a decision in a timely manner.

The solution is to break it down. Take that complex task and break it down to its bare essential components, and then tackle each one of those components one at a time. Gather the information you need. Write down the steps required. Then plunge into the task.

The hardest thing to overcome when you're trying to start something daunting and new is to actually start.

Some tasks are hard to contemplate for most people

— but fifteen minutes isn't. Fifteen minutes is manageable and can bring minor and major results, each one providing satisfaction and a boost in self-esteem.

### Reason 4: A lack of focus

The inability to prioritize and focus also contributes to procrastination. Those who cannot view the tasks at hand and place them into different categories based on their level of importance sometimes have difficulty getting anything done because they are constantly switching from one task to another or trying to decide what to do next.

Distractions are another major cause of procrastination. Distractions are everywhere. You must learn to ignore them. Sometimes, the temptation to engage in conversation with your coworkers, play games, or do other non-work related tasks can be a source of procrastination.

If you do not have any personal goals set, then it is almost certain that you will be lacking in focus, as you had no target to work towards. You may simply feel as if you are just drifting through life. A good goal encourages you to take action because you do not want to disappoint yourself by failing to achieve what you set out to do.

Try making a list of all of your tasks and ranking them in order of importance. Then, set a goal of completing two sets of fifteeners. After thirty minutes, evaluate your progress and reassess the situation based on the remaining tasks.

Whatever it is, all you need is fifteen minutes, and before you know it, some weeks later, you have accomplished a task you couldn't bring yourself to start.

Minimize distractions by secluding yourself. Disconnect the Internet and switch off your cell phone if you have to. Check e-mail and voicemail at set intervals instead of randomly every few minutes. Find a quiet space where you can concentrate on the task at hand. Only take breaks as a reward for accomplishing smaller sub-tasks. Setting up your workspace to minimize distractions and scheduling time to converse with your coworkers will help to prevent procrastination and keep your project on schedule.

**Reason 5: Low energy levels**

Some of us have relatively unhealthy lifestyles. Whether you get insufficient sleep or your diet causes you to feel sluggish and tired, lifestyle factors can play a huge factor in how inclined you are to get off of the couch and take action.

If you are always tired, it is hard to focus, and obviously you will not feel like doing much at all.

If you want to be active and productive but simply lack the physical energy to do so, then you are probably suffering from low energy levels.

The way out is to experiment with sleep, diet, and different peak times during the day, as well as an exercise routine in order to find a balance that works for you. There is a wealth of useful information online about making healthier lifestyle choices — and you've probably already got a fairly decent idea already of what changes you could make.

If you still don't get any positive results in terms of raising your energy levels, then consider consulting a health-care professional, in case there are underlying causes of low energy that require medical treatment.

**Reason 6: Perfectionism**

Another common cause of procrastination is perfectionism. You may suffer from excessive perfectionism if you find it difficult to take action unless you know you can do a job with which you will be totally satisfied. This also becomes a problem when you have to try something new, or different from what you are used to.

I think it was Albert Einstein who said that a person who has never made mistakes is a person who has never tried anything new. If you never tried in the first place, then you've got nothing to show for it at all.

It's one thing to be proud of the work that you do and to want to do your best. However, when your mental picture of something you want to complete is actually beyond what you can reasonably expect to do, then you have a problem. Basically, you know that you won't be able to do as well as you want...so it's easier to do nothing at all.

It's impossible to steer a parked car.

The main way to get out of this rut is to admit to yourself that your idea of perfect may not be someone else's idea of perfect. Aim to do your best and learn to be happy with the output, especially if it is achieved in a reasonable time frame.

### Reason 7: Fear of the outcome

Sometimes, we're afraid we'll fail. At other times, we're subconsciously afraid we'll succeed because we are fearful of the consequences of our achievements.

Maybe you fear that if you do well, then next time even more will be expected of you. Or, perhaps succeeding may place you in the spotlight when you prefer to be in the background.

This is a hard thing for many of us to admit, even to ourselves. But it may be what's keeping you from doing a job you need and really want to accomplish. If you can identify your reluctance as fear and track it to its source, you can deal with the fear and get on with the job.

Often, people fill out their schedules with busywork so that they have a "legitimate" reason for not getting around to the more important/frightening tasks. The fact is, that fear won't go away. But if the goal or outcome is worth pursuing, you'll be able to act in spite of the fear.

Excessive stress can increase this fear and lower productivity even more. Rather than committing to an excessive number of tasks in a short time, start out with a shorter list of tasks and gradually add items. You should prioritize the tasks that are the most important or time-sensitive. Overestimating or having high expectations is only more likely to be counterproductive. Therefore, another way out could be to lower your own expectations.

Now that we have examined the top 7 reasons for procrastination, let us look at the rules for the "7 Big Rocks Fifteener System"

# RULES

Now that we have identified the red flags, you might have a much better idea of what your reasons for procrastination are. It is now time to take a deep dive into one possible solution, which I refer to as the "7 Big Rocks Fifteener System."

There are six basic rules to make the Fifteener System a success.

#1. The listed tasks should be simple to complete.
#2. The listed tasks should not be "calendar items."
#3. Using a checklist is mandatory.
#4. The tasks should all be important — that is, things that matter.
#5. The tasks should all be placed in the right context.
#6. It is possible to combine multiple tasks as long as it does not take more than 15 minutes to  complete the entire checklist.

Let's look into these rules in detail:

### #1. The tasks should be simple to complete

If you have to think about each task as you set about doing it, you will probably end up not doing it at all, or exceed the allotted time and get frustrated. For example, a chef trying to come up with a new dish should not include it in the checklist; however, if he or she is making a dish that takes less than 15 minutes to create and has done it many times before, then it is reasonable to include it as a task.

### #2. They should not be "calendar items."

The 7 Big Rocks Fifteener System does not cover tasks that are date-sensitive or time-sensitive, such as a friend's birthday party or a doctor's appointment.

### #3. It is important to use a checklist.

The idea behind using a checklist is that the tasks should flow from one to the other. Using a checklist will help you perform tasks sequentially and efficiently. While certain tasks belong together, others don't; therefore, you should try to do them in a logical order until that logical flow becomes a habit.

### #4. The tasks should all be important — that is, things that matter.

Prioritizing is an important aspect of productivity. Listed tasks should be things that matter: things that are in alignment with your objectives and do not distract you from what you really should be doing.

### #5. They should be all placed in the right context.

If the checklist has multiple tasks, each task should be placed in the right context; for example, one should list together those tasks that can be performed at the same place.

### #6. It is possible to combine multiple tasks as long as it does not take more than 15 minutes to complete the entire checklist.

The main disadvantage of combining multiple tasks in a fifteener checklist is that you can feel overwhelmed very quickly. However, whether all the tasks are done or not, it is important to stop when 15 minutes are up to prevent the brain from coming up with excuses not to do these tasks in the future.

Use a simple kitchen timer that will go off when 15 minutes are up, and then just stop! Even if you are in the middle of a task! This will prevent the procrastination devil from coming up with reasons not to do the tasks.

# PLEASURE VERSUS PAIN

While I have always tried to be productive, there were some things I was lazy about even though I knew I should have been doing them. One of them just happens to be writing.

I had always put off writing books because I thought I was suffering from writer's block. I would start a book, write a few chapters, and then leave it halfway. This cycle changed when I read a book by Mark LeGrand Messick where he mentioned understanding the "why" behind my writing.

*"Why am I writing a book, when I could be doing something else instead?"*

This is the question I asked myself. I wrote up a list of reasons why I needed to write this particular book and I pinned it up on my desk. This served as a reminder of why I needed to finish this book.

In the past, another method that worked for me was the "pleasure and pain" principle. All humans do things either to gain pleasure or to avoid pain. If you are thinking about that delicious hazelnut-flavored cup of coffee, served along with a slice of rich chocolate cake with a dollop of ice-cream and chocolate sauce, it is obvious that you associate pleasure with food. The result? You order the dessert. On the other hand, when the alarm rings, if you are thinking about how difficult it is to drag yourself out of bed, find your running shoes, change your clothes, find your keys, and get out of the house to head off to the gym, it is obvious that you associate pain with exercise. The result? You hit the snooze button.

If you have a decision to make, list down the pain points of doing it and the pleasures of doing it. Let's assume that your problem is that you are not able to make it to the gym three times a week. What are your reasons for not doing that?

Grab a sheet of paper and draw a line down the middle. At the top of the sheet, write "Gym Workout." On the left side, write "Pain," and on the right, write down "Pleasure."Under Pain, write down all the reasons why you dislike doing it, and under Pleasure, write all the reasons why you want to do it. Chances are that the Pleasure list will be shorter than the Pain list. You can pin up your Pleasure list over your desk or at another convenient spot where you will see it every day. The Pain list would be the starting point for the Fifteener method.

Fifteen minutes a day to execute important tasks will take your life to the next level. That is the promise of this book. To do this, we need to make checklists of the sequence of activities we need to do. A fifteener checklist works for five out of the seven types of procrastination mentioned earlier. It may not work if the problem is excessive perfectionism or a lack of commitment. Similarly, there may be other reasons for your procrastination that I may have missed and would perhaps be better uncovered by a mental health professional if you are unable to pinpoint the reason on your own.

Is it possible to have a fifteener for cooking a dish? Yes, it is possible, provided:

#1. The ingredients/pots/pans are ready and assembled.
#2. The *miseenplace* (French for pre-prep) is done.
#3. The cooking time for that dish does not exceed 15 minutes.
#4. The recipe is handy.
#5. You actually like cooking and want to cook.

Here the words miseenplace/ pre-prep refer to the peeling and cutting of onions, filleting the fish or weighting out your flour etc which are not really part of the recipe but are tasks that get in the way of a smooth work-flow if you don't do them beforehand.

Even if you like cooking, you might find that you

are quite lost when you try to cook a dish you are familiar with in someone else's kitchen, especially if the person who lives there is not around to guide you.

If you know your way around a kitchen but have forgotten a key ingredient for your dish, either you have to settle for creating a different dish out of the remaining ingredients or you have to head back to the store to get that ingredient.

If you take each of these seemingly unrelated points together, you realize that your procrastination may just be the sum of these events. This would make it more exasperation rather than procrastination, but if you took away these pain points, you might actually have a chance to beat your procrastination once and for all.

I refer to these points as POP's (points of procrastination), and if you would like to zap your Procrastination Devil, your best bet is not massive action but instead small "zaps" of action. These zaps, or bursts, of action will give you the momentum to form new habits and routines, which will in turn reduce and eliminate your procrastination in your identified areas.

The system itself is fairly simple:
#1. Visualize the procrastination event as a series of steps.
#2. Quickly write down all the steps in the series of events.
#3. Next, visualize how you would like things to actually happen.

#4. Write down your vision from Step3.

#5. Write down the ingredients (what you would need to buy or collect)

#6. Figure out the number of checklists you would need, since each checklist should not take more than fifteen minutes to execute.

### Case Study

We will follow the journey of Steve, our protagonist from my first book, *CrazyBusy*, as he figures out how to use the Fifteener System. It helps to view problems from a third-person perspective, so taking a peep into Steve's world will enable you to customize the system to fit your own life.

### About Steve

Steve is a project manager in a high-tech company that creates Internet-related products for an international clientele. He is engaged to Sue and is doing very well at work. However, his life is far from perfect.

One of the problems Steve is facing is the fact that he only goes to the gym once a month! He decides that he needs to make it to the gym at least three times a week and decides to write down his reasons for not making it to the gym in the morning

Steve decides to try out the 7 Big Rocks Fifteener System so that he can zap his procrastination.

Before writing down his reasons, Steve visualizes what happened that morning and writes down his reasons for not making it to the gym:

*I did not get to the gym this morning because…*

(1) I can never find my shoes in the morning.
(2) I don't feel like doing it.
(3) I went to sleep late last night.
(4) It is difficult to navigate the bedroom in the darkness.
(5) I can't find my keys in the morning.
(6) I tend to wake Sue, who prefers to wake up later.
(7) I can't find my water bottle and towel.

He then visualizes how he would like his morning routine to ideally flow. He visualizes waking up with the alarm without hitting snooze, and then taking the flashlight and gently getting off the bed without waking Sue. After finding his slippers, he heads to the bathroom. He changes quickly and grabs the gym bag and keys on his way out the door.

As per the Fifteener System, he notes his "ingredients":

*I need the following things in the morning…*

(1) Flashlight
(2) Gym Bag
(3) Shoes

(4) Towel
(5) Water Bottle
(6) Keys

Steve realizes that he does not need to buy any of these things, but he needs to keep them handy.

He decides to create two checklists. The first list would need to be done the previous evening so that everything is ready in the morning when it is time to leave for the gym.

So, the first checklist would be as follows:
# Put the flashlight next to the pillow.
# Pack the shoes in a plastic bag and then put it into the gym bag.
# Put the socks and the towel into the gym bag.
# Put the water bottle into the bag.
# Keep the bag near the door.
# Hang the gym clothes on the hook in the bathroom.
# Ensure that the keys are on the hook next to the door with the car keys.

The second checklist would be executed as follows, when he is back from the gym:
# Keys go back on the hook as soon as I get in.
# Socks and towel go into the washing machine.
# Bag goes back into its place.
# I head for a shower.

It is important to note here that Steve's first

checklist is really about getting things into the right context or placement and chunking tasks together so that he can execute them effortlessly as he moves from one activity to another.

This brings us to our next chapter, where we discuss the finer points of "the context."

# THE CONTEXT

There are certain tasks, like writing a book, that require me to sit at the computer. So, if I were making a checklist for things to do while sitting at the computer, the computer becomes the context. In other words, the work is dependent on me having access to a computer, without which that particular checklist is useless.

**Keep all tasks grouped by location.**

This is something I learned from David Allen. The context goes beyond location, though. The context could refer to the time of day or place or resources required in order to complete a given task. Using the same example of writing a book, I require a computer for writing a book, but I don't need an Internet connection while writing — I just need one when I am editing the book. So the task of "write book" could go on the Offline Computer list while the task "edit book" could go on the Online Computer list.

When I was explaining the concept of "the context" to a friend, he replied "does that mean that you take a single list and break it up into multiple lists?" The simple answer to that would be "Yes" but the thinking behind this concept is much more profound.

Let me explain this further. Let's say you have a random checklist of twenty tasks, there is a very good chance that not all of those twenty items would require a computer to execute. Some of them might be physical tasks, such as, boiling an egg. It would not make much sense for you to execute tasks in a purely sequential manner, such as, getting up to boil an egg (task 2) after sending an email (task 1) and then coming back to the computer to execute task 3, which might be replying to comments on your blog.

It would be much better for you to club the computer based tasks together and keep the kitchen tasks on another checklist. This would enable you to move from one task to another without interrupting your work-flow.

By creating different lists for different contexts in your day, you will also prevent the long thinking process that hinders each step. You only need to look at the task list for a specific place or area, and you can then complete each task on the list without faltering.

During your breaks, you may refer to your lists and decide what to do according to whether you have the right tools or if you are in the right location. You will save quite a bit of time by organizing things this way. If you are on the way to the mall, you can simply grab the mall list on your way out to see what can be done while you are there, without worrying about the other lists. You will be able to move directly to the task that needs to be done rather than having to make decisions constantly.

# THE FISHBOWL METHOD

Another possible solution to beat your procrastination is the "fishbowl" method. A fishbowl can be used to store checklists or fifteener items for easy retrieval. The general idea is to bring in an element of surprise while ensuring that the system does not get too cumbersome to follow due to multiple checklists.

Advice for choosing this method:

#1. Communicate ahead of time with anyone who may inadvertently disrupt your fishbowl setup. This could include kids, your roommates, or the cleaning lady.

#2. Make sure that the physical space permits a fishbowl setup.

#3. Make sure that the fishbowl is within easy reach and not out of sight.

#4. Combine the fishbowl method with a kitchen timer to make it more effective.

**Case Study**

It has been two weeks and Steve has started going to the gym on a regular basis. He thinks that if the Fifteener System worked for the gym, it might work for other activities too, so he decides to take it further.

Instead of a fishbowl, Steve finds two plastic jars, which he labels "TODO" and "DONE."He starts out by checking out his home office for things to do. He notes that the office desk is a mess and decides to note that down as a fifteener. He also decides to file some papers in his filing cabinet and notes that down as a separate checklist. He moves on to the other rooms of the house and notes pending items such as Sue's birthday party guest list, shoes needing polishing, etc.

He now has quite a few folded checklists in the first jar marked "TODO," so he decides to get cracking and do two fifteener routines today. He sets his kitchen timer for 15 minutes, picks out one checklist at random from the jar, and gets cracking on it. After he is done, he drops the checklist into the "DONE" jar.

Steve keeps dropping checklists into the "DONE" jar as he goes about his daily routines. At the end of the week, he is surprised to note that the "DONE" jar is looking quite full while the "TODO" jar is almost empty.

He empties out the "DONE" jar and looks for

checklists that might need to be executed again and puts them back into the "TODO" jar. He throws away a few of the "done" checklists and files away some of the others that he thinks he could require later.

Over time, he notices that he never needs to do more than two fifteeners a day and that he has now made a habit of dipping his hand in the "TODO" jar whenever he has time to spare.

# PUTTING IT ALL TOGETHER

## Identify your life's Inboxes

David Allen, in his book *Getting Things Done*®, refers to "life inboxes," which are places where your information collects, such as the email inbox, postal mailbox, or voicemail. It can also help to have a physical inbox at work, so that colleagues know exactly where you want them to leave memos, notes, and so on.

The same principle can be applied at home, with all family members leaving you messages in the same place. The key is to keep the system simple, which makes it easier to implement.

I refer to these inboxes as "gathering points." A gathering point is any place where you gather "unprocessed" items. Things like email, tasks, to-dos, ideas, assignments, projects, or postal mail. The reason they are unprocessed is because you have not yet clearly decided either what to do with it, when to do it, or where its "home" is.

### Decide on processing times for each Gathering Point.

The best way to deal with each gathering point is to allocate a set amount of time and deal with all the entries in one go. This prevents you repeatedly checking the inbox and wasting time. It also allows you to spend the bulk of your day working on the tasks you are meant to be dealing with.

The frequency of checking may depend on your job, but generally, two or three times a day is sufficient for email and voicemail. It is surprising just how much time you can save over the day by simply limiting your visits to your email.

### Process each of your life's Gathering Points.

Whatever inbox or gathering point you are dealing with, you need to work methodically. You should assess each message and decide what to do:

**1. Trash it.** Make the decision to get rid of it and stick to that decision. Generally, if you don't have time or interest in a particular email right now, you won't at a later date, so delete it. If in doubt, you can always create a folder for "unsure" messages so they are removed from daily view but are still accessible.

**2. Deal with it.** If it will only take two or three minutes to complete, then carry on. Respond to it or forward it to someone who can. Deal with whatever the issue is so you can trash the item and get it out of your inbox.

**3. Assign it to a list.** For longer items, you should assign them to either a fifteener list or a project list. Then, create a time when the list is dealt with.

### Case Study

Steve has been trying to get a handle on his "inboxes" for a while now. He takes a week to consciously monitor and note down the many inboxes he has in his life. At the end of the week, he is shocked to note that he has a total of 32 inboxes at home and at work. He has three gathering points in his car itself — one on the seat next to him, another in his glove compartment, and a third in his trunk.

He decides to have no more than nine gathering points:

#1. A reasonably large physical "home inbox" for papers, receipts, magazines, etc.
#2. A portable leather folder
#3. A notepad
#4. A personal email inbox

#5. His smartphone
#6. His physical "work inbox" for the office
#7. A work email inbox
#8. His weekly review worksheets
#9. His two fishbowl jars

He decides to use the upcoming weekend to clear out all the 32 inboxes into the new gathering points. Unfortunately, it takes two weekends for Steve to finally have everything in the new inboxes, but he is very happy with the fact that his life is decluttered.

# CORE HABITS

In Chapter 4, I introduced you to the rules governing the "7 Big Rocks Fifteener System." However, the rules only represent one part of the system. There is also a second element called habits. The rules work in conjunction with the habits to make it a system. Everyone has both good and bad habits. Good habits can be hard to form, while bad ones can be hard to break. However, if you understand how they actually work, then you can make them work for you.

Charles Duhigg, a writer, talks about three different aspects involved in creating a habit. He calls them the *cue*, the *routine*, and the *reward*.

#1. The cue is what triggers your brain.
#2. The routine may be a mental routine, a physical routine, or an emotional routine.
#3. The reward helps the brain to decide whether or not that habit is worth remembering.

Your brain is being led by the habit. You acknowledge the cue, you follow the routine, and you receive the reward. A habit is life-altering, even if the reward is something that we know is bad for us; hence, we need to retrain the brain to break bad habits.

I have explained how a habit operates, but it is never too late to change your ways. Learning how habits work will give you greater insight into how to break bad habits to regain control of your life.

Habits are astonishingly powerful, and we must accept it will always be difficult to break bad habits. However, given time, virtually any bad habit can be broken.

### The Structure

# Identify the obsession.
# Isolate the cue.
# Experiment using rewards.
# Create a plan.

A simple example could be the phone ringing. Some people compulsively pick up the phone every time it rings. It takes a lot of effort to escape that conditioning. They don't give themselves permission to ignore the phone call.

Would you like to exercise more? Select a cue for yourself, like waking up in the morning. You can try visiting the gym right after waking in the morning.

Then, add a reward to that cue, like maybe having a smoothie after your workout. Begin to imagine that smoothie and the excitement you feel when you get it. Build up the anticipation of that reward. It won't be long before the craving makes it much easier for you to push yourself down to the gym every morning. (If your reason for exercise is to lose weight, then the smoothie may not be the best reward, unless it is a healthy smoothie.)

When you create a plan to break a bad habit, it can fail sometimes. The important thing is to debrief yourself by writing down the things that went well and the things that did not go to plan. The things that went well are important because you need to catch yourself doing something right and you can identify triggers for the bad habits by noting down the sequence of activities when things did not go to plan.

It is always easier to start with small situations and actions than to try and deal with larger and more complicated ones. This will come in time, but it is better to have the reward of increased productivity and the general sense of improved wellbeing that can be garnered from small changes to then fuel your motivation to make larger changes.

A simple example may be your email inbox. If you are sent an alert every time a message arrives, then the base impulse is to check immediately. If you cannot, then it remains on your mind and distracts you from your work. But likewise, if you do stop to check, you have also been distracted from your work.

So after assessing the situation, you might decide to turn off your email alert and decide on a couple of timeslots during the day when you will check and then deal with all your mail. Initially, you may have to fight the temptation to check mail, but after a few days you are more likely to feel the relief and reduced stress that comes with a simple change. By streamlining your work to prevent constant interruptions, you will also have reduced your stress and improved your productivity. This is a great start with any personal development strategy and an example of how your reaction to a simple situation can easily be changed.

Some of us require a little more direction before we can change. I have some habits that I have formed over the years, like:

#1. The Collect Habit
#2. Clean Desk Habit
#3. Action Habit
#4. Reward Habit

**1. The Collect Habit.** This habit involves carrying around a small notebook. As you go through your day, write down ideas, tasks, projects, and anything else noteworthy that runs through your mind. This takes it from your head to the paper so you won't forget it.

**2. Clean Desk Habit.** A good example of behavior change is making sure your desk is cleared off at the end of the day, and that each day you start off with a clear, clean desk. People easily fall into the habit of leaving their desks all cluttered and piled up. The next day, when they see it, it immediately evokes the tired feelings from yesterday. It causes stress and lowers productivity. Small changes can make a world of difference in your life.

When you are working on your computer, it is important to clean up your desktop to help you focus. The more clutter you have in your browser, on your desktop, and in your physical surroundings, the more difficult it is to really focus.

When you are in the kitchen, it is important to clear up all the pots and pans in your work area and your stove to ensure you are focused there, as well.

**3. Action Habit.** A lot of people have problems trying to make money online. They spend way too much time studying and learning all about marketing, reading forums, buying ebooks, and testing out new methods. They get caught up in the learning when what they should be doing is implementing what they've learned. Take action. You are free to make mistakes — that's how you learn. Get in the game and DO SOMETHING. Don't try to learn everything by just reading about it.

**4. Reward Habit.** Once you have reached some specific milestones and short-term goals, it's important for you to reward yourself. Reward is crucial to your success in changing habits. Stopping to take breaks is a proven way to increase productivity. Many people still hold to the idea that stopping your work means less productivity, and they are very wrong.

It's just like a computer. When you leave your computer on too long and have too many applications open, it will show signs of slowing down and you might need to reboot the computer or close some applications. It's the same with people. We all need to let go of things, even if it's just for a few minutes of rest. Then, we can be refreshed and go back and tackle them again. It replenishes your energy supply, both physically and mentally.

You may want to review the habits you have formed over the years by reviewing them in terms of the following categories:

# Health Habits
# Thinking Habits
# Emotional Habits
# Money Habits
# Shopping Habits
# Business Habits
# Motivation/Productivity Habits
# What time the habits occur
# Location-based habits
# Something you're doing or about to do
# Something you've experienced or are experiencing
# Urges

Some sample triggers/cues for you to consider:

# Health Triggers
- WHEN I need a boost of energy
- WHEN I get sick

# Thinking Triggers
- WHEN I have a negative thought
- WHEN I need to choose what to do next
- WHEN I take notes

# Emotional Triggers
- WHEN I experience failure
- WHEN someone gives me a compliment
- WHEN I meet someone new

# Money Triggers
- WHEN I pay my bills
- WHEN I get the urge to buy processed/junk food
- WHEN I get the urge to buy something

# Shopping Triggers
- WHEN I need to make a buying decision
- WHEN I enter a sales situation

# Business Triggers
- WHEN I enter a meeting
- WHEN I start a new project
- WHEN I need to give a presentation

# Motivational Triggers
- WHEN I'm bored
- WHEN I feel depressed

# Time-based Triggers
- WHEN my alarm goes off
- WHEN it's 9pm
- WHEN I get ready for work

# Location-based Triggers
- WHEN I enter my house after work
- WHEN I visit a new restaurant

# Something you're doing or about to do
- WHEN I take a shower
- WHEN I sit down to eat

# Something you've experienced or are experiencing
- WHEN two important things are competing for my time
- WHEN I wake up in the middle of the night

# Urges
- WHEN I get the urge to check my email
- WHEN I get the urge to click a link online

## Case Study

Now that Steve has decluttered his life, he starts out

with a compulsory fifteener to process his physical inbox daily.

Before he starts the fifteener routine, he allows himself a second to catch his breath and consider the reasons he wants to change by reading his list of goals aloud. He also notes that certain times in the day work better for fifteener routines. On holidays and weekends, he used to nap in the afternoon; however, he found he was able to do a few fifteener routines instead of napping.

At the end of the day, when he is back from the office, he makes a habit of dumping the contents of his portable folder into his physical inbox. He allows a few minutes at the end of each day to assess his achievements and to outline what needs to be done the next day. This gives him a much-needed head start the following day.

Starting out with these smaller habits has given him the motivation to make further positive changes in his life, and he rewards himself by taking Sue out for a surprise dinner.

Sue has noted that Steve has started picking up after himself in the last two months and is suitably impressed.

# MAINTAINING PRODUCTIVITY

It is one thing to get started on the "7 Big Rocks Fifteener System." It is quite another to maintain the momentum. This can be a challenge for many people. Even when you know what needs to be done, things get in the way. Disruptions and interruptions are unavoidable and a common part of everyday life. People call. Emails come in. Things get scheduled for you, sometimes without your even knowing. You get distracted and sometimes knocked off course.

And it's not just other people who get in our way. Sometimes, we get in our own way, like when we procrastinate on something challenging, something important, perhaps without even knowing why, pushing it off, letting other things take its place.

One way to keep from being derailed is to have a backup strategy in case of new challenges that arise. I call this backup strategy my "when-then" plan.

**The When-Then Plan**

If we forget to nurture our good habits, our inner saboteur takes over. This Procrastination Devil generally becomes stronger with time. A good when-then plan will help you zap your procrastination by nurturing your good habits. Getting back into the "good" old routine is challenging, but with a when-then plan, it is possible.

As an example, a good when-then plan can be written down as follows:

**WHEN:**
I get the urge to check email

**THEN** I will:
- Ask myself: Is this the most productive use of my time right now? **THEN**, I will:
- Delay taking action on the urge for just 15 minutes. **THEN**, I will:
- Dip into my fishbowl for something to do for those 15 minutes. **THEN**, I will:
- Set the kitchen timer for 15 minutes. **THEN**, I will:
- Do the fifteener routine.

I will admit that this when-then plan does seem overly simplistic, and a common objection I have encountered while helping people is that they have a problem getting started with it because their lives are overly complicated, so they don't think a simple solution to nurture their good habits will work.

So the first step, according to me, would be to simplify your life by trying out the following:

- Watch less TV and read more.
- Drive less and walk more.
- Shop less and spend more time outdoors.
- Focus on the present, not so much on the past or the future.
- Avoid noise and choose solitude and quiet.
- Play more and work less.
- Don't forget to breathe slowly and consciously.

## Case Study

Steve and Sue are now back from a short vacation. Unfortunately for Steve, he notes that his system seems to be falling apart. At work, there is a ton of pending items that have been waiting for his action, while at home he is quite lost with the piles of laundry and postal mail and the sheer volume of tasks clamoring for his attention.

He decides to create a when-then plan to get back on track. He realizes that the vacation has taken him out of his normal set of habits, his flow, and his frame of mind for getting things done.

He starts off by identifying the cues/triggering factors that are pulling him away from his normal fifteener routines. He realizes that when he finishes work at the office, he is always in a rush and just shuts down his computer and makes a run for his car. This looks like a great place for a when-then routine.

He writes down his when-then routine as follows:

**WHEN:**
- I end my workday

**THEN** I will:
- Review what I accomplished today, writing down a short, bulleted summary of each accomplishment. **THEN,** I will:
- Plan tomorrow's tasks. **THEN,** I will:
- Place my planned tasks where I will see them first thing tomorrow.

After a few days of following the when-then routines, Steve is back on track and is happy to process his unprocessed items down to zero almost every other day.

*As a reminder, "unprocessed items" are items lying pending in your inboxes since you have not yet decided what to do with them, when you are supposed to do them, or where you are going to store them. (Simply Google the words* "Inbox Zero" *for more information on this topic.) While the topic is more geared towards your email inbox, it can be applied to any inbox/gathering point.*

He now needs to re-look at his filing cabinet at home, because while processing his inboxes, he has created some backlogs of work for himself by filing away things to do at a later date. Some of these items are due now, so Steve decides to set up an appointment named "Clear filing cabinet" for every Tuesday and Friday, and automates this using Google Calendar so that it sends him a reminder twice a week.

A few weeks later, Sue surprised Steve with a brand new filing cabinet to replace the one he had. He was pleasantly surprised and asked her what the occasion was. She replied that observing him going about his daily routines was a pleasure, and that the new filing cabinet seemed very apt since he was so organized and efficient nowadays. Steve in turn surprised her by baking a cake for her the next day.

Steve managed to get Sue hooked on to the Fifteener System, too. This little system worked almost on autopilot, with occasional check-ins by either one of the partners to ensure the other one was on track.

# FIFTEENER SYSTEM VS. POMODORO TECHNIQUE

When I first started telling people about my FifteenerSystem, a few of them told me it sounded similar to the Pomodoro technique. This technique involves dividing a goal into 25-minute workloads. After 25 minutes of work, the person takes a five-minute break. After four cycles of this, the person is given a 15- to 30-minute break.

The Pomodoro technique helps in two ways. First, it trains a person to get used to following a schedule. So if a person makes a weekly plan, he's more likely to follow it. Second, it teaches a person the value of both work and play. Long breaks dull the mind, whereas long work hours exhaust the body.

Of course, the Pomodoro technique won't work for everybody or every job. For example, a chef can't apply the technique because taking a five-minute break will make him burn his onions. Every person has his own method or version of taking a break.

I usually write my books in 25- to 45-minute blocks, using the Pomodoro technique. This works well since it is more of a mental rather than a physical task.

The real differences between the FifteenerSystem and the Pomodoro technique are in sequence and focus. The FifteenerSystem is about chunking tasks together into a logical sequence where one task naturally follows another, thus creating a habit, while the Pomodoro technique is more about focusing on or immersing oneself in one activity for a set period of time.

For me, a fifteener is ideal for something like getting rid of clutter, winding up my workday, or a morning ritual to start my day. The best way to get started with fifteeners is to just give them a try rather than over thinking.

# CONCLUSION

The path of procrastination leads us to the opposite of where we want to go. It leads to more stress, less satisfaction, more frustration, and less fulfillment. The truth is that no matter how great you are at managing your time, the Procrastination Devil always rears its ugly head.

You've now learned the entire system — what it is, why it works, and how it works. Now, it's time to put it to use in your own life and business.

To help get you up and running quickly, here's a simple three-step action plan:

# Step 1: De-clutter your life by minimizing your gathering points.

# Step 2: Take two jars and create your fishbowl checklists by noting down fifteeners for the following.
#1. Your health, food, exercise

#2. How you start and end your day
#3. Controlling urges and bad habits
#4. Productivity/getting things done
#5. How you manage your emotions and emotional responses
#6. How you manage your money

# Step 3: Every week, choose one bad habit that is causing you to procrastinate and review that bad habit every evening by visualizing the sequence of events leading up to this bad habit. At the end of the year, you will have zapped 52 bad habits that are causing you to procrastinate!

Now you are equipped with all the tools to "zap your procrastination." Keep or replace any of the methods as you see fit. Just remember that the overall goal is to keep things moving so that it does not get too monotonous.

Zapping your procrastination is a choice. Until you consciously and intentionally catch yourself procrastinating, you will always be accomplishing things that don't matter.

I wish you all the best in your life journey.

www.ingramcontent.com/pod-product-compliance
Lightning Source LLC
Chambersburg PA
CBHW070943180526
45168CB00003B/1160